PICTURE LIBRARY

SATELLITES

PICTURE LIBRARY
SATELLITES

N. S. Barrett

Franklin Watts

London   New York   Sydney   Toronto

© 1985 Franklin Watts Ltd

First published in Great Britain
   1985 by
Franklin Watts Ltd
12a Golden Square
London W1

First published in the USA by
Franklin Watts Inc
387 Park Avenue South
New York
N.Y. 10016

First published in Australia by
Franklin Watts
1 Campbell Street
Artarmon, NSW 2064

UK ISBN: 0 86313 226 X
US ISBN: 0-531-04948-5
Library of Congress Catalog Card
Number: 84-52002

Printed in Italy

Designed by
Barrett & Willard

Photographs by
British Telecom
NASA
Novosti

Illustrated by
Janos Marffy

Technical Consultant
Robin Kerrod

Contents

Introduction

Hundreds of satellites travel in space around the Earth. These are man-made, or artificial, satellites. They are taken up into space by rockets or by the Space Shuttle.

The Moon is also a satellite of Earth, a natural satellite. This book is about artificial satellites. There are many different kinds, used for different purposes.

△ Engineers prepare a large communications satellite for launch aboard the Space Shuttle.

Satellites are expensive to make and launch, but they do important jobs.

Communications satellites carry radio, TV and telephone signals around the world. Weather satellites help to forecast the weather. Scientists use satellites to study the Earth, planets and Sun. Some satellites are manned by astronauts.

△ Two small satellites in the cargo bay of the Space Shuttle. Satellites may be launched into space by the Shuttle and placed in orbit around the Earth. Or they may be launched directly into orbit by a rocket.

7

Parts of a mapping satellite

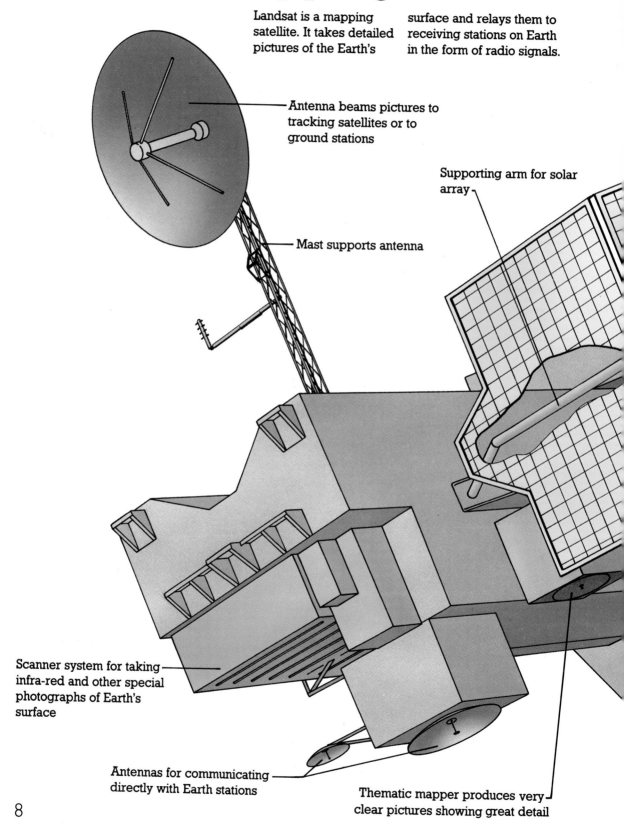

Landsat is a mapping satellite. It takes detailed pictures of the Earth's surface and relays them to receiving stations on Earth in the form of radio signals.

Antenna beams pictures to tracking satellites or to ground stations

Supporting arm for solar array

Mast supports antenna

Scanner system for taking infra-red and other special photographs of Earth's surface

Antennas for communicating directly with Earth stations

Thematic mapper produces very clear pictures showing great detail

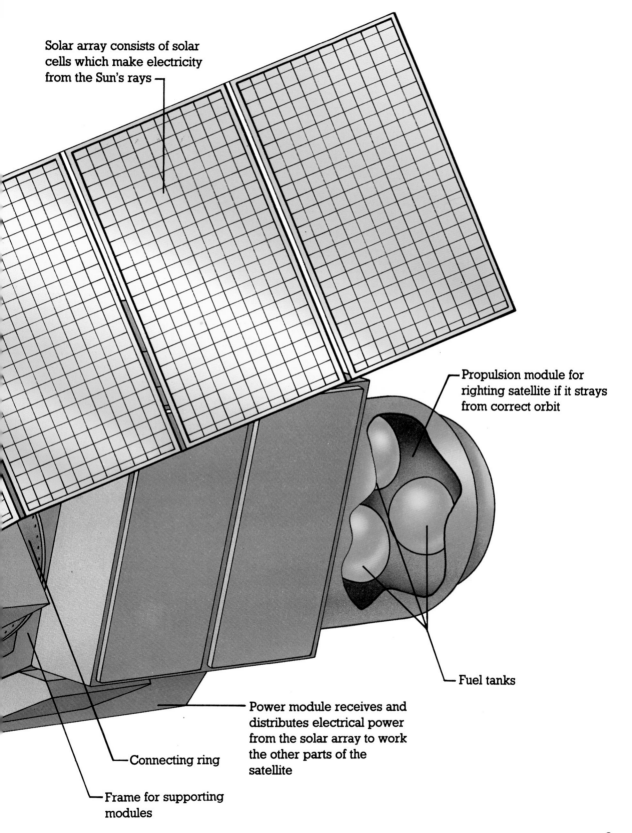

Solar array consists of solar cells which make electricity from the Sun's rays

Propulsion module for righting satellite if it strays from correct orbit

Fuel tanks

Power module receives and distributes electrical power from the solar array to work the other parts of the satellite

Connecting ring

Frame for supporting modules

9

In orbit

The path a satellite takes around the Earth is called its orbit. Some orbits are nearly circular. Others are oval, or elliptical.

Powerful rockets are needed to send a satellite up into orbit. The satellite has to travel very fast to avoid falling back to Earth, but not so fast that it escapes altogether.

△ A communications satellite spins slowly out of the Shuttle's cargo bay. It must travel at just the right speed for its orbit. It has small gas-fired jets that can put it back on course if it drifts out of orbit.

Communications satellites

Many satellites have been sent up to relay, or pass on, signals around the world. These are called communications satellites. They receive radio, TV, telephone or other signals from ground stations. The satellites amplify, or strengthen, these signals and then send them back to Earth, to another ground station.

▽ INTELSAT V, one of a series of international communications satellites. The "wings" are solar panels. They use the Sun's rays to make electricity to run the satellite.

Most communications satellites are positioned in space so that they are always above the same spot on Earth. This is called a stationary orbit.

In fact the satellite is moving very fast. It goes around the Earth in exactly 24 hours, the same time it takes the Earth to revolve once. So the satellite appears to stay in the same place.

△ European Communications Satellite (ECS) is a communications satellite that relays television programmes across the world.

Communications satellites travel in a very high orbit above the equator. They can connect ground stations a long way apart. Just three satellites, in orbit over the oceans, can serve most of the world.

Signals travel with the speed of light, so they can reach the other side of the world in a split-second.

▽ Large dish aerials like this one send TV signals to communications satellites.

Experiments in space

Scientific satellites serve many purposes. They might carry special instruments to study the Earth's magnetism, for example. Some satellites study rays from the Sun or outer space.

Information is often recorded on tape and played back to a ground station when one is in range.

△ The Solar Maximum Mission Satellite (SMMS), designed to study the Sun.

▷ This giant satellite is known as the Long Duration Exposure Facility (LDEF). Nearly 200 scientists from around the world contributed to some 50 experiments carried in the LDEF.

Predicting the weather

Weather, or meteorological, satellites help scientists forecast the weather. They take TV pictures of the clouds as they move through the atmosphere.

They can provide advance warning of storms, and have saved many lives. Ships sometimes use the information from satellites to avoid dangerous weather conditions.

▷ A satellite picture of cloud cover over western Europe and the Atlantic.

▽ GOES-D is one of a series of satellites launched to give early warnings of violent storms and to track the path of hurricanes. It also collects weather information from thousands of automatic ground stations.

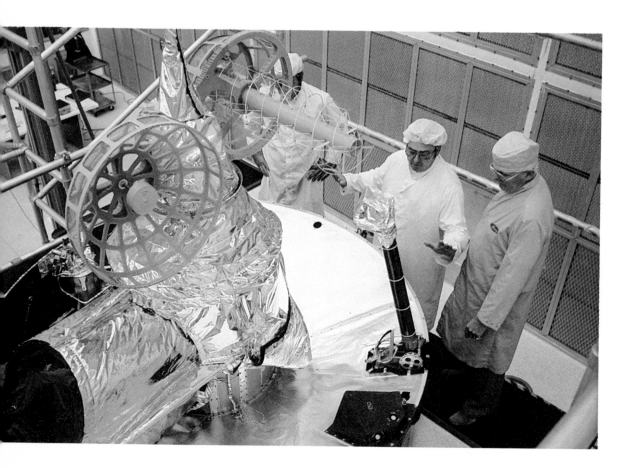

Studying the Earth

Spaceflight has enabled us to learn much more about our own Earth. Special satellites are used to map the land and oceans in great detail.

These satellites can also help scientists make surveys of resources such as forests or minerals. Their cameras can produce special pictures that show healthy vegetation and diseased plants in different colours.

▽ A satellite's view of Death Valley, in the western United States. This scene was produced by the special thematic mapper on Landsat-4.

Studying the heavens

Telescopes on Earth are limited because the atmosphere blurs our view of the heavens. The orbiting astronomical observatory (OAO) is a satellite equipped with telescopes and measuring instruments. It radios information back about outer space. Other, more powerful, space telescopes are being planned.

△ The Space Telescope, planned for launching into orbit by the Space Shuttle in 1986. Its mirror was unveiled in 1984.

Satellites in space

Spacecraft called probes travel to the planets. Some probes are sent into orbit around the Moon or planets and become satellites.

Russian Luna and American Lunar Orbiter probes became satellites of the Moon. American Mariner and Viking probes became satellites of Mars.

▽ The picture shows how the American space probe Mariner 9 became the first satellite of Mars in 1971. The low point (closest to Mars) of its elliptical orbit took it near the moon Phobos. The high point took it close to Deimos.

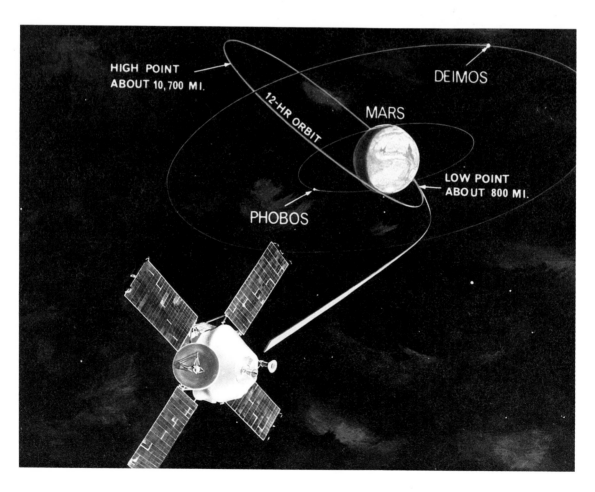

HIGH POINT ABOUT 10,700 MI.

DEIMOS

12-HR ORBIT

MARS

LOW POINT ABOUT 800 MI.

PHOBOS

Tracking satellites

Satellites are controlled from Earth. They carry radio transmitters to send out signals. These are picked up by tracking stations or ships, which send signals back.

In this way information is transmitted to Earth and the satellite is given instructions by signals from Earth.

△ A Russian tracking ship, the *Vladimir Komarov*, named after a cosmonaut who died on a space mission. Both the US and the USSR have a large network of tracking stations on land and sea for collecting information from satellites.

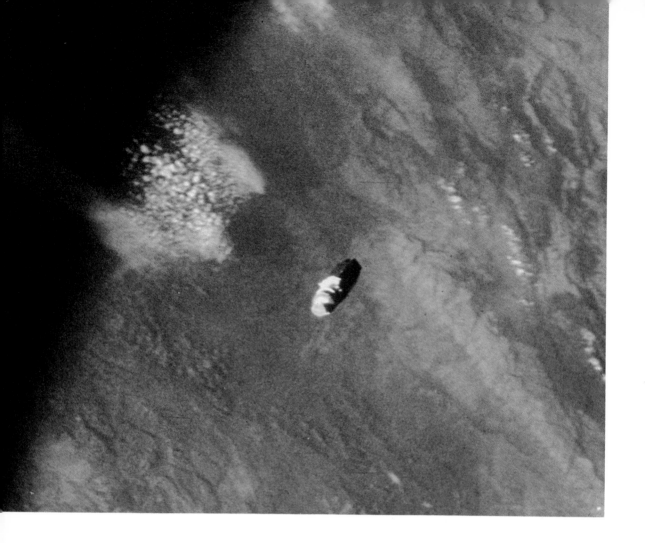

Satellites may also be tracked by other satellites, such as the TDRS (tracking and data relay satellite). These satellites, which are part of a special system, relay information to a ground station.

The TDRS system is used not only for tracking ordinary satellites. It is also designed to cover all Space Shuttle flights.

△ The TDRS after separation from the Shuttle, with the Earth in the background.

▷ The TDRS takes up most of the Shuttle cargo bay.

Manned satellites

Manned spacecraft in orbit, like the Space Shuttle, are also satellites, even if only for a few days.

Space stations, such as Skylab, are special kinds of Earth satellites. They allow many people to live and work in orbit for long periods. The Russians have launched several Salyut space stations into orbit. They work with Soyuz spacecraft.

▷ The Skylab space station, launched by the US in 1973. Astronauts travelled to Skylab in Apollo spacecraft. This orbiting laboratory and workshop was launched by a Saturn V rocket.

▽ An astronaut works on the outside of Skylab.

◁ A plan for an American space station to be built by the mid-1990s. Whatever the final design, the space station will be built in stages and serviced by the Space Shuttle. A Shuttle orbiter can be seen at the bottom right of the picture.

The space station will be in Earth orbit and will always be manned. The Shuttle will bring changes of crew.

The story of satellites

Sputnik

Earth's first artificial satellite was Sputnik. It caused a sensation when the Russians successfully launched it into orbit in 1957.

Sputnik circled the Earth in $1\frac{1}{2}$ hours. It sent back simple "Bleep, bleep" radio signals. Sputnik marked the beginning of the Space Age.

△ A model of Laika, the first space traveller, in Sputnik II.

Dog in space

Russia soon launched Sputnik 2. This was a much bigger satellite, and carried a dog called Laika which became the first space traveller. Unfortunately, Laika died in space, because there was no way to bring the satellite back.

Explorer

The first US satellite was Explorer I, launched in January 1958. It discovered important belts of radiation in space around the Earth.

Famous firsts

The US satellite Vanguard II was the first to send weather information back to Earth, in 1959. In April 1960, Tiros I took the first detailed weather pictures.

The first communications satellite was Echo I, launched in August 1960. It was a big silvery balloon, about 30 metres (100 ft)

△ Tiros I.

△ Engineers check out Echo I, the first communications satellite. It was a large "balloon", which folded out of the round metal container at the top of the launch rocket.

across. Echo was a passive satellite, which means it did not send out signals. Signals were bounced off it from one ground station to another.

Telstar I, launched in July 1962, was the first satellite to relay TV programmes between the US and Europe. It was also the first privately built satellite.

Early Bird
In 1964, 14 countries set up a group called INTELSAT (International Telecommunications Satellite Consortium). Their first satellite was Intelsat I, or Early Bird. Now there are more than 100 nations in the group and dozens of Intelsat satellites have been sent up.

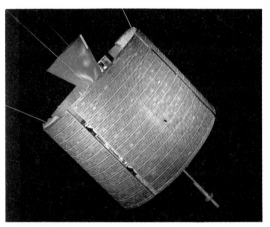

△ Early Bird.

Star Wars
Many satellites have military uses, including spying. Spy, or reconnaissance, satellites are used to photograph enemy forces and weapons. Warning satellites guard against missile attacks.

Both the US and the USSR are developing satellites capable of shooting down guided missiles with lasers, just like in the film *Star Wars*.

29

Facts and records

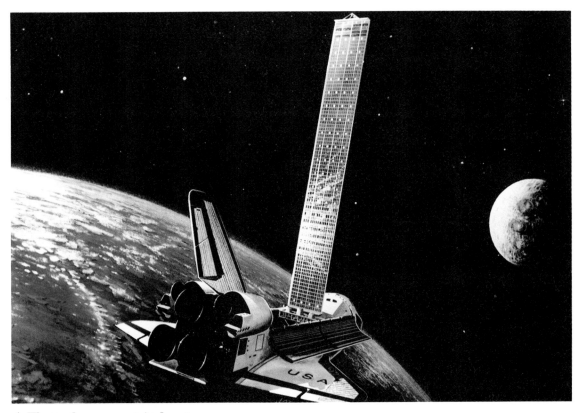

△ The solar array tried out on
Discovery's first mission.

Shapes of satellites

Satellites can be any shape,
depending on their job. They do
not have to be streamlined like a
plane, because there is no air in
space.

Silent satellites

When a satellite's batteries go
dead or its electronic equipment
breaks down, it cannot transmit
signals. It just circles silently until
it finally falls to Earth.

Solar cells

Satellites depend on solar cells
for the power to keep them in
orbit. Tests are in progress on a
solar array big enough to power
the Space Shuttle and keep it in
orbit for a month or more.

On Discovery's first flight, a
dummy solar array was tried out.
This amazing panel folded out
from the cargo bay to a height of
31 m (102 ft), greater than that of a
10-storey building, all from a
folded stack only 7.5 cm (3 in)
thick!

Glossary

Atmosphere
The layer of air that surrounds the Earth. Beyond the atmosphere, space begins.

Communications satellite
A satellite used for relaying signals between ground stations a long way apart.

Intelsat
A partnership of nations whose Intelsat satellites form a world-wide telecommunications system.

Landsat
The Landsats are a series of satellites used for mapping the Earth and studying resources such as minerals and food.

Meteorological satellites
Satellites that collect information about the weather.

Orbit
The path a satellite takes around the Earth or another body.

Passive satellite
One that does not send signals but is used as a "mirror" for reflecting or "bouncing" signals from one Earth station to another.

Probe
A spacecraft sent to explore bodies in space, which sometimes becomes a satellite of one body.

Reconnaissance satellite
One used for photographing enemy forces and weapons; also called a spy satellite.

Solar array
A set of panels on a satellite consisting of solar cells that face the Sun and make electricity from its rays.

Space station
A large manned satellite that people live and work in for long periods.

Space Telescope
A large telescope to be launched by the Space Shuttle in 1986. It will be able to see much farther and produce very much clearer and sharper pictures than any telescope on Earth.

Stationary orbit
A satellite in a stationary orbit takes exactly 24 hours to go around the Earth, so it always appears to be above the same spot on Earth.

Index